Yeme
Eating

Gwenyth Swain

Turkish translation by Fatih Erdoğan

MILET

LONDON

For Vinnie, who loves to eat!

To find out more about the pictures in this book, turn to page 22.
To find out more about sharing this book with children, turn to page 24.

The photographs in this book are reproduced through the courtesy of: Stephen Graham Photography, front cover; ©Elaine Little/World Photo Images, back cover, pp. 9, 18; IPS, p. 1; ©Gerald Cubitt, pp. 3, 20; Sharon Wilharm, p. 4; ©TRIP/C.C., p. 5; ©TRIP/H. Rogers, p. 6; ©TRIP/M. Peters, p. 7; ELCA photo. Used by permission of Augsburg Fortress, p. 8; David Chittenden, p. 10; George Washington Carver National Monument, National Parks Service, p. 11; SeaQuest Cruises, p. 12; ©TRIP/F. Good, p. 13; F. Botts/FAO, p. 14; Eliot Elisofon, Eliot Elisofon Archives, National Museum of African Art, Smithsonian Institution, p. 15; Jeff Greenberg, p. 16; WPF/FAO photo by F. Mattioli, p. 17; ©Lyn Hancock, p. 19; ©John Elk, p. 21.

Eating/Small World Series

Milet Limited
Publishing & Distribution
PO Box 9916, London W14 0GS, England
Email: orders@milet.com
Web site: www.milet.com

First English-Turkish dual language edition published by Milet Limited in 2000
First English edition published in 1999 by Carolrhoda Books, Inc., USA

Copyright © Carolrhoda Books, Inc., 1999
Copyright © Milet Limited for English-Turkish edition, 2000

ISBN 1 84059 143 9

Typeset by Typesetters Ltd, Hertford, England
Printed and bound in the United States of America

Kahvaltı zamanı. Ne yiyeceksin?

It's time for breakfast.

What will you eat?

Sütlü mısır gevreği mi?

Will you put milk on cornflakes?

Yoksa tatlı bir meyva mı?

Or will you grab something sweet?

Bazılarımız yerken biraz dikkatsizdir,
Eating can be messy.

bazılarımız da çok eğlenir.

It's also fun to do.

Ellerini yıka ve şükret.

Wash your hands. Give thanks.

Sonra da haydi başla.
Then dig into your food!

Kimimiz masada yer,
You can eat at a table,

kimimiz yerde,
on the ground,

kimimiz de ayakta.

or on the run.

Ama yemeye başlamadan önce yapacak ne çok iş var.
But before you can eat,
there's a lot to be done.

Yiyeceği satın alırız, ya da üretiriz.
Buy food or grow it.

Sonra ayıklarız.

Then, pound it or sort it.

Doğrarız, karıştırırız.
Chop it, then stir it.

Fırına koyarız, ya da tencerede haşlarız.
Grill it on a fire or cook it in a pot.

Yiyeceklerin tadı nefistir; kimi acıdır, kimi tatlı.

Food tastes great—sometimes hot,

sometimes not.

Yiyeceğimizi paylaştığımızda hem tatları
paylaşırız, hem de güzel anları.
When you share a meal,
you share good tastes and good times.

Şöyle bir oturup, koca bir ısırık aldığımızda...
Sit right down. Take a big bite!

İyi hissederiz kendimizi, karnımız
yavaş yavaş doyduğunda.
Eating will make you feel just right.

More about the Pictures

Front cover: Peanut butter on bread makes for fun but messy eating for this boy in Ann Arbor, Michigan.

Back cover: A girl in the Philippines carries a big bowl full of bananas.

Page 1: Two boys in Guyana, in South America, slurp flavoured ice cones.

Page 3: For this toddler in northern India, breakfast starts with a bottle of milk.

Page 4: This young girl in Cantonment, Florida, begins the day with a bowl of cornflakes.

Page 5: At a market in Toluca, Mexico, children eat sweet, ripe bananas.

Page 6: In Scotland, a toddler tastes—and wears—chocolate.

Page 7: Two English schoolgirls stop for a spaghetti lunch.

Page 8: Young children in Hong Kong say grace before eating.

Page 9: These boys in Morocco, in northwest Africa, use their hands to eat couscous topped with vegetables and meat.

Page 10: Women on a trip to Antarctica eat lunch on their ship.

Page 11: Kids on a field trip to the George Washington Carver National Monument in Missouri take a lunch break.

Page 12: A student on the go in Ho Chi Minh City, Vietnam, eats a quick snack.

Page 17: Women in Ghana, a country in West Africa, make smoked herring on a grill.

Page 13: In Puttaparthi, India, a boy brings home a basket of tomatoes to cook.

Page 18: At a shelter for homeless children in Bangkok, Thailand, children get a hot meal.

Page 14: A teacher shows off the vegetables she has grown in Malawi, a country in southeastern Africa.

Page 19: A teacher in Fort Simpson, in the Northwest Territories, shows native Canadian girls how to make hot dogs covered with bannock, a kind of bread.

Page 15: A woman in Nigeria, in West Africa, removes cocoa beans from their pods.

Page 20: A child from a hill tribe in Tamil Nadu, India, sits down to eat.

Page 16: It's time to chop onions in this kitchen in Chisinau, Moldova.

Page 21: In Paris, France, a mother and son share some mealtime fun.

A Note to Adults on Sharing This Book

Help your child become a lifelong reader. Read this book together, taking turns as you both read out loud. Look over the photographs and choose your favourites. Sound out new words and come back to them later for review. Then try these "extensions"—activities that extend the experience of reading and build discussion and problem-solving skills.

Talk about Eating

All around the world, you can find people eating. Discuss with your child the kinds of foods people eat in different countries. Where do you get the food you eat? Where do people in other parts of the world get their food? What ways of preparing food are shown in this book?

Make a Food Chart

With your child, draw pictures of the foods you both love to eat. Find pictures of your favourite foods in magazines. Then find out where your favourite foods fit on the food pyramid. Which of your favourite foods should you eat less of—or more of—in order to be healthy?

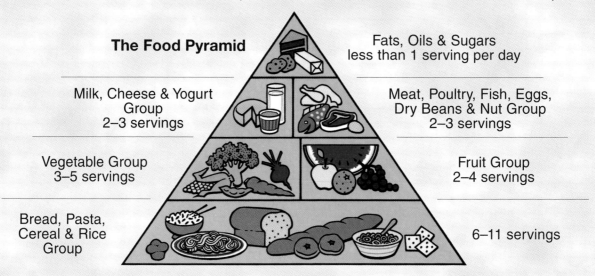

The Food Pyramid

Fats, Oils & Sugars
less than 1 serving per day

Milk, Cheese & Yogurt
Group
2–3 servings

Meat, Poultry, Fish, Eggs,
Dry Beans & Nut Group
2–3 servings

Vegetable Group
3–5 servings

Fruit Group
2–4 servings

Bread, Pasta,
Cereal & Rice
Group

6–11 servings